Midsummer

a poem

Glen Armstrong

Contents

I

It's warm and loud
    But few complain

I dream in unpredictable fits
    And starts

The teenage girls
    Turn cartwheels on the lawn

While their boys
    Smoke designer marijuana

Someone makes a sexual joke
    About the beast
    Of burden's load
    But few laugh

Likewise, most of the fireworks are duds
    So the children light

    Each other's fuses
    They fuss

    With openings
    Fashioned to pass fire

    From atmosphere
    To powdery heart.

II

Flames and mayflies
    Give way to brighter days

    Explosives and bugs
    Big enough for their own middle
    Initials

The famous couple walks
    Ignoring the absurdist's
    Ugly walking stick

They kiss and life goes on
    Though no one is sure

    Of the method or manifesto
    The shape the unbalanced

    Heart takes

Still the town continues
    To study love

    Examining the traces
    Of wedding cake
    On songbirds' talons

Though the gathered musicians
    Try to honor all requests

No one remembers
The chord changes

To "Cherry Pink and
Apple Blossom White."

III

Violence done beyond dirt roads
    Dirty rides taken

    A family name
    And its dangling chain

There's a place where Grandfather
    Crosses

    Out the names of his enemies
    A locked cedar box

Another with his Audubon
    Bird cards

    The flamingo bent
    Into a painfully beautiful
    Truce between science and art

Part of me needs the old man's blessing
    Permission to marry
    That girl with the bewitchingly fertile voice

There is no love
    However
        Without restriction
        Or physical discretion
        If you'd prefer

We must always lay each other down
    Within the confines of

    A bed / a city / a poem
    A Roman orgy

    A phone book / a sense
    Of smell / the hell

Passed down to us

    Lemon-yellow gloves / a broken
    Trust / the water
    Tower's shadow / that cramped space

    That awkward pose
    That displays the entire body.

IV

Wild canaries return
    To neighborhoods
    Bordering the cannery

That flat grey horizon bubbles
    Up aroused by a yellow wing

They all sing and they are
    All beautiful

    So connected
    I fear
    To the natural world

    That they can only be understood
    By this distance between
    Myself and them

I am the unnatural

    Amazed by a song that falls
    From the sky

A white shirt dries
    On the clothesline

    The warmth of a midsummer day
    So different
    From the warmth of a bare breast

Barely there at all even when myth
And memory conspire
To make it so

A low flying plane interrupts the flow
   Of something

I would almost call nature

If not for my fear of falling
If not for my fear of song.

V

Nature has its vein of gold
　　Cheese its bleu network

This feeling will never survive
　　Without a secret hiding place

The bee has its hive
　　Mind its subconscious
　　Face its subcutaneous tissue

On has its off
　　The cough drop box
　　Its odd bearded brothers

　　Cod its liver oil
　　Hat its tin foil

Lonely alchemists hide
　　In the alley

　　The only place
　　Their ongoing research on hiding
　　Makes sense

South of here

There is work being done in the canebrake
　　On the afternoon shadows
　　Cast by silos

Expose any aperture
    And that other world
    Starts whispering.

VI

She comes walking down
    The street
    Just
    About midnight

And the tightly woven strands that distinguish
    Sidewalk from song
    Open up a bit

    Van Morrison's voice nothing less
    Than a sleeper cell

    Armed to tear into elsewhere
    As the disc jockey awakens it

My grandfather heard only noise
    No urgency

    He couldn't hear
    The other world

    That these rock
    And roll singers
    Had been to

With its disproportionate emphasis

    On locked green doors

Hats where none were needed
And baldness

Where none was expected.

VII

Information the shadowy trees
    Might have

    Can be coaxed with a feather

    Love is ticklish
    Feathers abound

We gather more than we expected
    Damp leaves
    Stuck to our thighs

    An old
    Mylar birthday balloon

    Philosophical arguments
    Between fingertips
    And ticket stubs

Consider the nature of nature as
    Revealed at the movies

    Where this season's zombie takes
    Another bite of thigh meat
    Ill met / helmet / thighs meet

We listen again to the trees
    That can't help but cast
    Their shadows into the theater's

Parking lot

Walking home the bullfrog
    Sings

The moon and the wind
    It longs for sing

A ring / coin / slipper
    Lost forever

The little man in the boat
    Sings

The little informant
    In the trees

    Flies off.

VIII

Celebrate

Oh celebrate the agitated
    Flakes of skin

Celibate

Our most satiated acts of love
    Are relative celibacy when compared
    To those in cola ads

Kindly chemists have gathered

    Enough rosebuds and musky linens
    Enough broken sandals

    Candles / scandals / happenstance
    Lubricant / Subaru / subterranean
    Impulse / crocus

They have invented new ways
    To be fey

New ways to be green
    New ways to be the midday sun

    Or a pedestal of fire
    Or a round of applause.

IX

The sky tonight
    Is like a correspondence
    Course in Shakespeare

I will play every part in the dream

Assume each point of view
    In the same brown shoes

    Each new moon
    Each new hat
    Each new boat

Treaties signed
    On neutral shores

    Sliced Asian pears for monsters

"Grrr . . ." growled her hair
    Parting itself to reveal a gun

When the play is done
    The work of termites resumes

    Sugar holes / bites
    White noise destroying
    The prop-master's satellite

And when the costumes are locked
        Back into their trunk

        The field mouse ears and tail
        Speckled with blood

        The magistrate's cape and instructions
        To the ladies

I am no one.

X

The boy wears a pair of men's white
    Cotton briefs

    There will be no debate
    On pee stains or any other mystery

    This is a baptism
    Nobody agreed to

As for the thespians performing
    Midsummer Night's Dream
    At the community center

    They too clutch the damp elastic
    Their little souls inhabit

We feel helpless
    We were all promised snow cones

Life's slow unwinding
    Will be acknowledged

    If by nothing
    Other than a cold
    Dark release into the water

We were promised some kind of afterlife

We leave our assigned seats
    Our place in line
    Upon the long walk

    Home nothing looks right
Something has died

We were promised
    An intermission
    But the story drags on.

XI

Something has washed its feet
    In my Diet Coke

Something sparkles and drowns
    As if surrendering
    To a need so ancient

        That *dream* is the only name
        We can offer it

        For now at least

In that smoky realm only hinted at
    By manhole covers releasing
    Otherworldly steam

        Dreams cannot be bought
        Sold / previewed / advertised

There must be something between the screen
    And projection booth

        Skin and love
        Showtimes and ticket sales

        Unreal enough to undo
        All expectations.

XII

I hand-paint bicycles at night

I've known the green but not the tree
    The dust kicking up
    In the distance

    But not the destination

It's easy enough to remove
    Rust / to give hope

I make those precise adjustments
    To leg braces that allow
    For summer breeze and libido

    Adjust the desirable piece
    Worth more than the whole
    Stripped bare by thieves

There are too many heart shaped gears
    I want to adjust the bride's

    perfect teeth

I must accept those dissonant
    But necessary chords
    that will make
    The song miscarry.

XIII

I pray that chance and quirkiness
    Keep my child from danger

That a disconnected line
    Be her smile

That she never befriend the girl
    On the milk carton

    Balanced and unblemished
    Who seems

        Forgive me

    To be the same child every time

That no computer program ever ages her digitally

    Considers her
    With a wider face
    Longer hair

    The small purple corners
    Of dimly lit rooms
    And cigarettes

    The birthmark under her training bra

A drop of milk makes its way
    From the spout to the opening
    Of her shirt

Rather let her spoil and ache
    For the world

    In her bedroom
    A wild pincushion of a girl

    Listening to Mozart
    On the public radio station.

XIV

Contrary to folktales
    The things they steal away
    While we sleep
    Are rarely missed

Just enough gasoline
    To make it over the border

Just enough lipstick
    To break up a marriage

The letter x and the shoe
    And the old man's tiny bathtub

They are fascinated by popular
    Music and strong language
    And adult situations

They hear our prayers

    And often laugh
    Out loud at our desires

    Their own fires hotter
    But contained in little capsules
    No bigger than poppy seeds

They are bored with the U.S.A.
    It's a mystery to them

Why statistically more songs
Don't rhyme "China"
With "vagina" or

"Cotton Mather"

with "soiled lather."

XV

You would assume me a nubile
    Caught up in an ever-shifting
    Pattern of bare legs and

    Shoulders / twilight / discolored
    Tooth of a beauty / ready

    To take my difficult place
    To serve my turn as *it*

        If I confessed to being aroused
    By flashlight tag

Or maybe a dirty old man
    But I am neither

I am stirred by iron gates
    Heavy weathered things
    Unquestioned and clamped
    Down for years

Though there was a time long ago
    When I moved as
    Gracefully as any unhinged
    Beam of light

Even then when the sun set
    I was hesitant

To dash from the tractor tire
Planted with petunias
For home.

XVI

Beautiful thing
        About the unknown
        Is that it knows
        No restraint

Our garden variety ghost
        Slips nature's shackles

        Its face
        A bag
        Of moan

                And pause

That weird cant

The point where language breaks
        To let the unusual
        Through

Creatures with bullets
        For teeth

The quiet one
        With the prominent ears

        Extends the pause

Does not
Want to be noticed

It's almost as if we know him

Through the rumored fog.

XVII

When we tired of sex and poetry
    We took inventory
    Of sail boats
    And redwing blackbirds

It was like catching stones
    Skipped from the other direction

    A dance upon the water / less
    Emptiness for a while

Nothing frightened us back then

    Though there were shadows
    That shouldn't have been

    Shoes that no longer
    Made sense

    And discarded baby names
    That raccoons made
    A mess of

Each red thread your kimono shed
    Hit the earth with a thud.

XVIII

This yellowed song is lovely and frayed
    Weary
    As its singer

A fly lands on the open hymnal
    His fate
    To be flattened
    Near a dotted half note

This song of praise is stained
    Prisoners have better skin

Its singer half insane
    Dreams of being locked away

The whole damn world has carved
    Insignia of a better designed
    More daring world

    Into its thigh

I've longed and jittered
    And pushed straight
    Pins through the abdomens
    Of quarter notes

    Never entirely sure
    If the ritual is doom
    Or preservation.

XIX

Because sleep comes on
    Like an ocean
    We sing our young a tide

    Melodies that ease
    Their little heads into the deep

    No steep mole or blind mountain
    No desert prophet

Because sleep is delivered
    By strange puppeteers

    Each afraid of the other body
    Obscuring hand or shin

We sing the children their escape

Lullaby and detonation

    Queer harmonies
    So subtle

    That each mother's voice
    Seems at once her own
    And something else

Because tomorrow's broken headlight
    Makes tomorrow night strange

Because song is never enough
　And sleep is not a choice.

XX

The poets and folksingers
    Who weave their parallel universe
    Have never heard of you

No naked foot
    Hastens upon its wings

No face brightens
    As your name is rescued from
    Muddled thoughts

Yet you breathe
    In and out
    Warm nothings

Owing legend everything

    Free to slip through windows / bricks
    Pines / sleepy witnesses

Saying nothing
    Maybe

    They dream

Staying nimble
    Saving your kisses for now.

XXI

We climb that narrow stairwell

>
> To sip wine
> And listen to music

Or to sip wine and ponder
>
> Some part of the sky
> That seemed until now
> Sufficiently understood

Or to sip wine as someone opens
>
> A window

We speak softly short
>
> Of whispering

>
> Sort of buzzed

>
> Sort of questioning
> These Saturday nights

We risk very little

>
> And still fall

>
> From the balconies

>
> Of toy buildings.

XXII

The brain can imagine itself
    Incarcerated by the skull
    Surrounded by a wall of bone
    Alone

    Reaching out
    Through the prison's
    Sensory cracks

Whispering in the dark

To another brain in a neighboring cell
    And even if

The brain is designed to fail
    At love

    And only advance as far
    As infatuation's security fence

    It makes do
    It imagines a mulberry tree

    It imagines a monster
    Protecting the face and naked

    Foot waiting patiently

    Dissolving / bleeding

    Into the landscape.

XXIII

Revealed to the artist
    In a dream

    And never
    Quite captured by daylight

The ink on his brush
    The curvature and virgin

    Bristol board that might

    Hail The Moby Grape
    The Quicksilver Messenger
    WSG to be announced

That which isn't real delights

    We must never say aloud
    That this is so

But the artist is just a man
    Dressed up as Ahab's
    Missing leg

Figment and fig leaf give way
    To line and wavelength

Don't fear the canvass
    Whispering

Don't be frightened
    As the whale slips out

    Of its costume.

XXIV

I wake up and each new day
    Has its own crazy voice

    I lose all sense
    Of continuity

    To make things worse
    Each moment wants to outdo / undo
    It's predecessor

I walk to the store
    Enjoying my shoes

Turkey potpies fulfill
    Their destinies

The cars and the cars and the cars
    Go by the cars

These fits and starts
    Counter my heartbeat

    I rattle apart

I am part of the day again
    Like a wheel

    And I tire

Each new moment more easily
Of gaps

That hint
Of loss.

XXV

In spite of the physical danger
        We ran half-naked
        Through the woods

Becoming stranger to each other
        The further we got
        From the city

Seeing ourselves for the first time
        Stripped from red wine's
        Vaporous vines

        And poetry's cleaner foot
        The sex manuals / the hymnals
        That denounce them

        The recipes for stroganoff
        The soft-focus lens

We countered western civilization's
        Slow fade from flesh

        Yet sentient cherries
        Continued to whisper
        Lines from *West Side Story*.

XXVI

I had something to say
    About the way a pretty girl
    Can change a city

    But I kept it to myself

I just smiled and twisted
    One of the charms
    On your bracelet so I could see
    It a little better

I didn't fit in and you told me

    That my past attempts
    At small talk
    Were uncivilized

I needed more time and a whole
    Second language to explain

So I drank and drank and imagined a wall
    Poster-bombed by the lovers
    Of a big gorilla hand

    Its mount of Venus
    Clearly traced
    By thick black ink

The more carefully I chose my words
    The more I dreamed
    Of unauthorized signage.

XXVII

Body glitter / Ray-Bans / baby
    Shrimp on plastic swords

    Confetti
    All over the sidewalk

    Like the guts
    Of a lovesick clown

This may be our last chance to scuttle
    Through the city's legs

What our fingers find half-
    Alive in the neon

    Streams endlessly
    The limo driver's lime

    Wedge / polyester
    Uniform / uninformed / undo

Unto the pending nuptials
    That which never let the household
    Cast its shadow

    A hang / over / hung / gargantuan

Our life together towers like a monster
    More threatened than threat

The rubber fang
The plastic tine
The promised tang
The spilled wine.

XXVIII

Short of snapping under the weight
    Of signs and symbols
    I must confess

    To believing in convergence
    Not necessarily

    Of planets / cats / fingers
    Four-leaf clovers

    Lavish paintings / street
    Dancers / lemon juice
    And Absolute

It's warm out / you linger

    At the fence in a torn tuxedo
    Dress shirt / cutoff jeans

    You signal a new era / error
    A green collage of lips

    Love's chance splicing
    Of youth / fashion / classic
    Science fiction

Later we might walk through streets both moonlit
    And canopied by cloud

Each thought expressed aloud

Each street

Each season.

XXIX

I could send my voice out
>   Into the world with its satchel
>   Full of folk blues

>   In search of a few beautiful sentences
>   A Japanese puzzle box

>   Defiled again
>   Telephone again
>   Sleeplessness

This world / parts of it
>   I strive to resist

>   Wear me down

I need coffee where my voice
>   Should be / be effective

I need liquor / an ear / an audience

>   Oh voice
>   You've always been
>   My favorite

>   Body part but the artless
>   Quarter you offer

>   My thoughts
>   Is criminal.

XXX

Afterwards there were questionnaires
    And parasagittal MRIs

    Some brains sparkled
    Like Christmas trees

    Some lit up
    Like a map of Athens

I don't remember much
    I think I cashed the check

    For participating
    In this study and spent

    The money on a copy
    Of DeSade's *Justine*

At one point she was running
    Through the woods
    With bruises on her thighs

At one point the situation
    Was so perverse
    That she slipped into
    Another dimension.

XXXI

All summer pretty girls have been living
    Surrounded by mysterious thoughts
    Drinking red wine

    In the city
    And we've forgotten
    Life before they arrived

It's hard to believe in survival

    Of the fittest
    When a twelve-hundred
    Pound cryptozoa is about

    To pound your face in
    And the summer girls

    Inspire the rest of us
    To take one on the chin
    For philosophy / sweet corn
    Peter Gunn / pity's sake

It's hard to fake this kind of eyelash
    Or that kind of fur

Many of them are said to thrive in shadow
    Many are cooler

    To the touch

Than the fantasies
Of grown men would have them

Imagine finding a book about the summer girls
    While walking
    Through dense
    Forest growth

    Or visiting a Buddhist temple

    Imagine a book bound in green
    Leather and divided
    By a ribbon placeholder

    And every speck of human
    Folly borne so far
    By the summer girls
    Is reaching out to you
    Grasping both sides
    Of your shirt collar

    It's almost as if
    Their collective hands
    Hold you accountable

Leave to the singers of modern song
    Their blood red skies

    And aftershaves

A transformation has taken place here
    Cleaner than a whistle
    And meaner than a she-wolf

Primal / feminine / disruptive
Alive in the recent transformation

Subtle / serious / elsewhere.

XXXII

We could dress up in gowns
    And get married

Dress up in wings and commune
    With owls

Undress
    bathe and towel off
    In the midday sun

We could straighten our ties
    And crunch numbers
    Until five o'clock

    Then come home to drink
    Martinis and crunch

    Colors and shapes until its time
    To once again start crunching
    Each other between the sheets

We could dress up as January
    February Canary and April

We could take a vacation
    And stay in a castle

We could dress as the floor
    That Julia's nightgown replaces

The empty room through which a single bodily hair
    Has its say

We could dress as fingers or legs
    And run
    Through the carefully
    Reconstructed ruins

    Looking for hands or torsos
    To hold us.

XXXIII

My child has her cape

The match its blue tip

The whisper never wanted
    Its cage
    (Its cage)

The whistle its rape

Theatrical lighting and sound
    Their low frequencies

And the audience is as shameless
With its hands as its hiss

There was a girl they all called
    Piss Queen

The sticky playbills all caught up
    In a makeshift twister

She drops her skull

Unlocks her teeth

But it's her shoes

    (It's her shoes)

    That make their point.

XXXIV

Wind through the trees
    Through the rustled nerves
    And just desserts / the just now

    Deserters

And the young woman's impossible
    Hair

The low rumble
    Of distant trains

    Sleeping crows and her father's
    Complete refusal

    To listen not
    Only to her
    But any snap

    Of a dry branch . . .

There is a kind of trance
    That the mystics warn against

A quickening
    Unfastening

    And crash

Her legs ache but she keeps pace
    At least for now with

Need / tree / season

Gloom / bloom / soon.

XXXV

On this cold stony planet
    With a hammer
    And a shoe

Some women read as statuary
    Some obscure themselves in trend

    The men muddying
    And bloodying hands and knees
    Make little difference

We improvise / we tighten

I watch her biting
    Her thumbnail

I plead to the satellite
    And women dance

    Their movement breaking free
    From their bodies

    Their moonlight superfluous

    Their quake unearthly.

XXXVI

I am not the wind
Nor would I ever choose
To be cold
A sensation I have known
In the past
Which only shows that I am not
Currently the wind
If the wind and the cold are one

But that largely imagined membrane
Separating the night
From my own unseen depths
Is thin

I hear a shotgun and some dogs
    Once again

    The philosophers refine
    Their tales
    Of stone and veils

Any cupped hand is a conduit
    Whether or not
    I agree to it

Whispers and distant shouts
    Make their way inside

And I am the wind
  The breath
  Caressing the kindling

  And fattening the *oh*.

XXXVII

To be the stirred air trilling

    With gossip
    The clippings carefully glued into

    A scrapbook
    Of sophisticated looks

To be every sentient beast
    On the planet slunk
    From its riverbed

    In time to sip tea

    To be Victorian and dried
    And yellow and so ashamed
    Of its legs

    That it only
    Putters about
    Its stately home

    (But to put most of this off
    To only slink for now)

To constantly think about skin

    Midtown
    Where perfume ads
    Shackle otherworldly nudes

To the page

To be alone and seventeen
And on the run

The clock / nightingale / cigarette

Streets and avenues named
After trees sway

Or after famous men
Where an old-timey plastic
Still prevails

To do these things and more is

To see with a fresher set of eyes
Two grapes that have slipped
Their peels

Baby teeth in a jar
Of Vaseline

A feeling that this has happened
Before / for the first time

To be words in a lovely mouth

We head south
And the world thickens

We meet and jelly / bone
Metal rail / aromatic

Automatic / tender / careful

Inching / itching
Worming out / warming up

Caterpillar's supposition / Amaryllis belladonna's

False promise to the carpenter bees.

XXXVIII

While I was silent and somewhere
    Between myself and all traces
    Of myself

You whispered sweet centipedes
    Into the jagged places
    I no longer occupied

It would be neither complete
    Nor inaccurate
    To call
    The nurtured fissures
    Sleep

In a lighter mood
    The world's creepy-crawlies
    Might be dismissed

    As nightmares

When the day breaks
    We will choose

    Between pet names
    And eviction notices.

XXXIX

Those who have borne the world
    Longer than I

    Who remember voices
    Where no song remains

    Who no longer flinch
    At the approaching fist
    Nor blush at tales of lonely sisters

    No longer make believe
    Nor abide the congenital cruelty
    Of fools

Those who envy us only
    Our troubled
    Sleep

    Exist

    By different laws of physics

    And define their struggles
    Through other legends

Sometimes on the way home
    They tip their fedoras
    Or ironically ask for the time
    Of which they

Of course
Have plenty / none

And in that season
Or some unknown reason
We dwell on them

Wondering into the night
Why they

Smelling of cough drops
And tasting of ceremonial smoke
And choking up the bones

Of deep ocean
Beasts
Extinct since lightning was king
Bother to even look our way.

XL

Her nose elevates
    The mood

As do the rude drawings

    Done to fill the border
    The hymnal / the boredom

Take care or take carelessness
    To new extremes

Some of us hear voices
    From beyond
    Filtered through the centuries'
    Phase shift module

It's more important
    To discuss

    The aftermath

Some of us transcribe
    What we hear
    Inventing little pencil cyclones
    To wash words away

Others roll naked in the morning dew
    Like dogs / like masters
    Of ecstasy / like minded

    Like bodies liking bodies.

XLI

How I envy the fey

    The blunt
    Explanations

    Offered up
    Just for them

    Their trajectories
    And wings

The glowing hair and unexpected
    Hairlessness

They care so little
    I don't believe

    They've ever seen a girl
    Twisting in her bed

    Every muscle denying
    The day and the day after

Laughter and sighs
    Too subtle

Cranes
    Swans and flamingos
The same / still

    They dazzle me.

XLII

It's only natural
    For the bell to be hollow

    Without rules or mind
    Or the world's warm breath

It rings
    We listen

Rarely taking the bell's savage
    Loneliness to heart

The sky is grey and silent
    In their beds
        Old men become their ears

Within the nothing the bell must be
    Designed with and defined by

    Is a hammer

    The bell lashes out
    From within

    Its every strike
    Reflexive.

XLIII

Upon returning to the city

The burning effigies
    And smoldering puppets

    Smiled from within
    The flame

Love of course
    Would have its day

The beer flowed and the pile of feathers
    Formerly known as a murder of crow

    Continued to grow
    Into the night

A light rain trickled down

We took questions
    From the gathered press

    And answered them
    As if unfolding origami birds

Midway through the school choir's
    Off-key song of welcome
    We retired for the night

In bed it was clear
    That our adventure
    Had damaged us

The open paths of skin
    We'd let each other travel

    Were as littered with monsters
    As any place on Earth.

XLIV

Again we become

The walls
    And should they hang

    Our portraits
    Upon us

    In artist's dreams
    Reintroducing us
    To ourselves in such
    A way

    That our unacknowledged

Sadness
    And charm

    Dance naked in the manmade
        Squares

    Where moonlight and window
        Throw themselves

        Onto the floor

We will be nothing
    More than a whisper
    In a hurricane

Nothing more than a night train
    With a broken whistle.

XLV

The old world persists
    In forgotten dance
    And pawnshops

Like a stubborn bit
    Of genetic coding

    A coarse and curly
    Satyr hair
    Still unwinding

That last sip of wine as well

I can feel the unspoiled lineage
    Of grape and strangle-weed
    At war in my throat

The orchestra runs empty
    Bottles up and down
    The cello strings

It's not so much fertility
    That our wedding guests

    Wish upon me and my bride
    As the weight

    Of the whole
    High kickin'
    Fertile world.

XLVI

We forever give up walking
    Down the street

We purchase a cuckoo clock

And help children polish rocks
    For the 4H Fair

Feathers / home teams / felt
    Scraps of pelt / flower / all

      But the most practical
      Fabrics have kissed
      Our hats goodbye

We no longer cry under
    Trees / umbrellas / ill-fitting
    Pajama tops

Soap dishes come
    And go

That tastiest / least poisonous
    Slices of fugu

      Remains near the little swimmer's heart
      It bumps up against
      Something more instinct
      Than regret

It watches its world
Puff up while we debate
Sentience

And regulate sashimi

We wear loose fitting robes
Around the house

Replace the couch cushions

How the youthful and stubborn
Have been undone

By such insignificant measures
Of time and comfort

We forever leave lust's hand-blown
Fixtures and ransom notes

For a photo album

So many shots of us
Pained by the pose

And the carnival attractions
The skeletons and devils
Decorate the dark ride
Eternally out of focus

Until the next generation's young lovers
Climb over these walls
That we've become

I'd like to tell you a story
　　　Both sad and dumb

　　　Where the telling is essential

A story where time
　　　Is the hero.

XLVII

Reportage becomes story
    Story legend

Before long the bloody war
    That captured our imagination

Is reenacted

Likewise the *facts of life*
    As the sixth-grade
    Health instructor calls them

    Turn wildly fictive
    Incubated in whispers

The girls on the playground
    Skip rope chanting

    As if to discredit a deity

      Miss Lucy has a baby
      It swims like a little fish

And the boys cut themselves
    Out of whales

The taste of blood and semen

Admittedly this
Seems a little advanced
For the school yard

But over the hill and far away

The village elders salvage zippers
From tuxedo pants.

XLVIII

I kissed a girl on a bus
    And that bus went everywhere

I kissed a girl with the windows open
    And the windows were our mouths

By this time the act of kissing
    Had gotten all muddled
    With the act of rolling

The landscape revealing itself
    Little by little
    Mile by mile by mile

Word got around
    And word got embellished

By the young
    Who would roll into each other
    With abandon
    Like dice warmed
    By the very thought
    Of a stranger's breath

By the dead
    Who had left instructions

    Their tombstones chiseled
    More beautifully

The inscriptions equal parts
Memorial and mystery

I could see the gears
Under those words

I could feel the globe's
Steady spin

Against my bare skin
My feet moist with morning dew.

XLIX

These dried and repainted particle board
      Representations of grass
      Speckled with wild violets

Look fine under the stage lights

Up close these props
      Have told too many tales

      Their wonder undone
      The chicken wire showing through

Times are tough in Michigan
      And someone had given me
      The ticket

For a little while
      I was warm and somewhere
      Else

I left both grateful for and confused
      By that city in a box

      Too shrill and insincere
      To lift me from my theater seat

      But certainly that much needed
      Elsewhere

For a moment
  The cast
  Stopped concentrating on lines

  And danced with such abandon
  That their chicken wire

  Glowed and burned beautiful
  Patterns through
  Their crudely applied makeup.

L

I need the old broom
    And the dustpan with the curled lip

I've never sipped wine
    Or engaged in polite conversation

People seem far too comfortable
    Undressing
    In front of me

This morning a talking bee
    Climbed out of the snow

    And whispered zzzzz
    At my window

I froze for a moment
    It's more a matter of empathy
    Than sanity

If anything can happen
    Then a flatness
    More sad than interesting
    Takes over the day

A little rip in the speaker
    Will make it seem like there's a leak
    In the music

Glittery black and white
    Indigenous to 1950s television

    The sky tonight is full
    Of conflicting fictions
    That all take place there

I consent to have my heart
    Beaten to a pulp

Some prefer the pulp

From here on out
    The crowd gathered around

    Thins and begins again
    When conditions are right.

Acknowledgements:

Sections of this poem first appeared in the following publications.

II	*Anti-Heroin Chic*
III	*Dirty Chai*
IV	*Eunoia Review*
V	*Altpoetics*
VI	*Elm Leaves Journal*
VII	*Avatar Review*
IX	*Bayou Review*
X	*Oddity*
XI	*Five 2 One*
XIII	*Fragments of Chiaroscuro*
XVII	*Minute Magazine*
XX	*Subprimal Poetry Arts*
XXIII	*63 Channels Magazine*
XXV	*Lunch*
XXVIII	*Eyedrum Periodically*
XXIX	*Ghoul's Review*
XXX	*Ygdrasil: A Journal of the Poetic Arts*
XXXII	*Sundog Lit*
XXXIII	*BlazeVOX*
XXXV	*InkStain Press*
XXXVI	*Ithica Lit*
XLIV	*White Stag*
XLV	*2 Bridges Review*
XLVI	*Subterranean Blue Poetry*
XLVII	*Impspired*
XLVIII	*Fine Flu Journal*
L	*Sweater Weather Magazine*